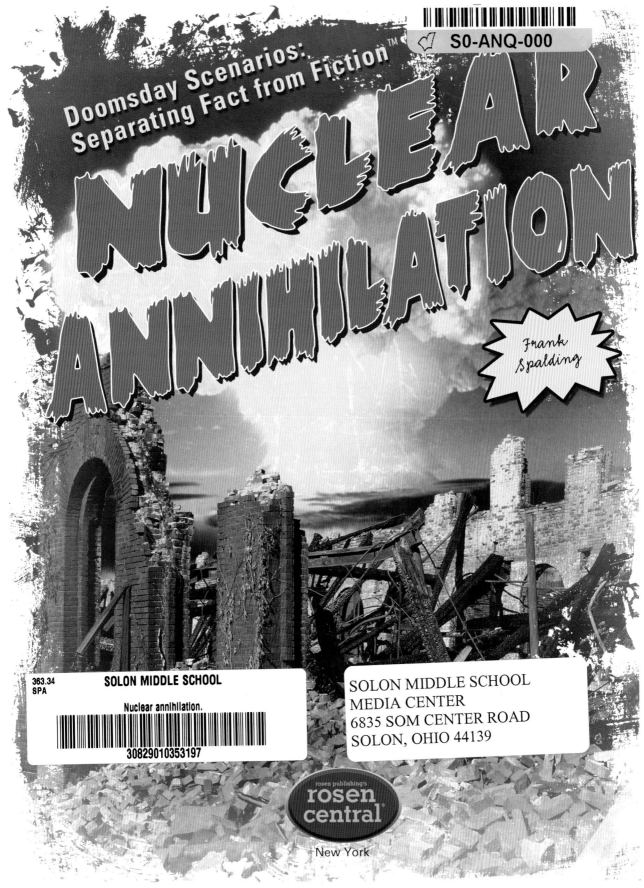

Doomsday Scenarios: Separating Fact from Fiction™

NUCLEAR ANNIHILATION

Frank Spalding

rosen publishing's
rosen central®

New York

For George—all of your dreams will come true. I promise

Published in 2010 by The Rosen Publishing Group, Inc.
29 East 21st Street, New York, NY 10010

Copyright © 2010 by The Rosen Publishing Group, Inc.

First Edition

Library of Congress Cataloging-in-Publication Data

Spalding, Frank.
Nuclear annihilation / Frank Spalding.—1st ed.
    p. cm.—(Doomsday scenarios: Separating fact from fiction)
Includes bibliographical references and index.
ISBN 978-1-4358-3560-3 (library binding)
ISBN 978-1-4358-8522-6 (pbk)
ISBN 978-1-4358-8523-3 (6 pack)
1. Nuclear warfare—Juvenile literature. 2. Nuclear weapons—History—Juvenile literature. 3. Nuclear weapons—Safety measures—Juvenile literature. 4. Nuclear disarmament—Juvenile literature. 5. World politics—21st century—Juvenile literature. I. Title.
U263.S68 2010
363.34—dc22

2009016685

Manufactured in Malaysia

CPSIA Compliance Information: Batch #TWW10YA: For Further Information contact Rosen Publishing, New York, New York at 1-800-237-9932

On the cover: The death and devastation that a nuclear explosion can wreak is almost beyond human comprehension. The detonation of a nuclear bomb can kill millions of people in the blast itself and through eventual radiation-related disease. It can turn areas surrounding ground zero into an uninhabitable wasteland for hundreds of years.

CONTENTS

Introduction

Five years from now, frightened American families gather in front of their television sets. An emergency news broadcast has interrupted the normal programming. According to the news anchor, an unknown terrorist group or groups have simultaneously detonated briefcase-sized nuclear devices in five cities around the world. Explosions in New York City; Washington, D.C.; London, England; Moscow, Russia; and Tel Aviv, Israel, have claimed the lives of thousands—possibly millions—of people.

Amid the confusion, worldwide intelligence agencies attempt to discover who detonated the bombs. More than a dozen terrorist groups claim responsibility for the action, but it's not clear who the culprit really is. Two of the bombs—those in London and Tel Aviv—were not full-on nuclear weapons but rather "dirty bombs." Dirty bombs are conventional (ordinary) explosives meant to spread radioactive waste.

The explosions in Washington have also claimed the lives of many members of the U.S. government, including the president. The vice president is in China on a

Members of a special Marine Corps unit conduct a training exercise. The exercise is designed to teach them how to respond to a terrorist attack on U.S. soil.

diplomatic visit. From thousands of miles away, the vice president tries to coordinate government agencies to offer emergency and humanitarian aid to New York and Washington, as well as to assess the danger from radiation.

People attempt to flee from the smoldering cities. The chaos and panicked crowds make it almost impossible for emergency services to help those injured in the explosions. Although the Pentagon has been destroyed, the U.S. military quickly works to restructure its chain of command. The Kremlin, Russia's seat of government in Moscow, has been destroyed.

Because of electrical disturbances resulting from the bomb going off in Moscow, the Russian military is unable to effectively coordinate its emergency response and national defense efforts. When Russian radar misidentifies a Finnish airplane entering its airspace as an incoming American ballistic missile, a Russian official initiates a nuclear strike against the East Coast. Intercontinental ballistic missiles soon leave their silos from a secret Russian missile base in the Ukraine. U.S. antimissile countermeasures only destroy some of the incoming Russian missiles. The remaining ones hit their targets, virtually destroying Boston, Albany, and all of New York City.

Fearing further attacks, the vice president authorizes a return nuclear strike on select Russian targets, including all large cities and military installations. While the missiles are in the air, the Russians launch a second round of missiles, intended to disarm America's missile silos. Newscasters report that the U.S. government is encouraging people to stay home and seek refuge in their basements. Other reports come in stating that Israel has launched a nuclear weapon at Tehran, Iran, and that India and Pakistan have begun launching their arsenals at one another.

After less than a day, the nuclear weapons stop flying. Most major cities in the United States have been destroyed. Hundreds of millions of people have been killed. Millions of others have suffered from horrific burns. Hospitals are over-flowing with patients, many of whom die before they can even receive medical attention. Millions of others are sick

Ever since the invention of nuclear weapons, people have been in awe of their tremendous and destructive power. As more countries get these weapons, there is a greater chance that they will be used.

from nuclear radiation. Radioactive dust and debris sent into the air from the nuclear explosions drifts on the wind, blanketing large parts of the country that had not been attacked by bombs and missiles.

The United States becomes eerily quiet. Many of those who did not die from the explosions die of radiation poisoning in the next few hours, days, or weeks. Those with working radios eventually learn that many of the world's major cities have been destroyed. Survivors are instructed to stay inside until the amount of radiation outside drops to a safe level. The news reports are confused: some mention riots in the cities that haven't been destroyed and that people are fighting over food and supplies.

The first survivors emerge from their shelters and see a bare, dead countryside. Dust and ash sent into the atmosphere from the bombs block the sunlight, causing an unnatural and unseasonable winter to descend over the land. Most major American cities have been destroyed. Bands of survivors roam the landscape, sickened and diseased and desperate for food and water that has not been contaminated by radiation, wondering if they will survive to see another year.

Could such a series of events actually happen? Could civilization as we know it be destroyed by nuclear weapons? What events would cause such a horrifying scenario anyway? How likely is it that we might face nuclear annihilation?

Chapter 1

THE EVOLVING THREAT OF NUCLEAR ANNIHILATION

Nuclear weapons are often mounted on long-range missiles like this one.

Nuclear weapons are the most destructive weapons in the world. Although a number of countries have them, they have only been used in an act of war once. Today, there are nearly twenty-four thousand nuclear weapons in the world. More than eight thousand of them are fully operational.

If these weapons were used in a nuclear war, life as we know it would change forever. Many people would be killed, and cities would be destroyed or made uninhabitable. Long-lasting environmental damage would affect Earth's forests, rivers, and wildlife. A full-on nuclear war would have effects so devastating that they are virtually impossible to imagine.

To truly understand the threat of nuclear annihilation, we must understand how nuclear weapons came to be invented—and how they were first used.

WWII and the Manhattan Project

From 1939 to 1945, the deadliest conflict in human history—World War II—caused the deaths of tens of millions of people. Many of those killed were civilians. The war was fought between two different factions. On one side were the Axis powers, which included Nazi Germany, Fascist Italy, and Imperial Japan. On the other side were the Allied powers, including England, the Soviet Union, and the United States. The goal of the Axis powers was to dominate the world. The Allies fought to stop them.

In 1939, physicists Leó Szilárd and Albert Einstein wrote a letter to U.S. president Franklin Delano Roosevelt. The letter warned Roosevelt that scientists had recently made a breakthrough by splitting the atom for the first time. They had discovered that when an atom was split, it released an incredible amount of energy. This could result in a process known as a nuclear chain reaction, which

Albert Einstein is one of the most famous scientists in history. He was one of the first scientists to recognize the possibility that nuclear fission could be used to create powerful weapons.

could create a very powerful explosion. Szilárd and Einstein thought that nuclear energy could be harnessed to create a superpowerful new weapon: a bomb capable of creating the largest explosion the world had ever seen.

At the time, the United States hadn't yet entered World War II. Many Americans believed that the war overseas was none of the United States' business. But on December 7, 1941, Japanese planes attacked a U.S. military base in Pearl Harbor, Hawaii. The United States could no longer remain neutral.

In 1942, President Roosevelt initiated a program to develop the most powerful weapon in history. The program, known as the Manhattan Project, was led by the brilliant physicist J. Robert Oppenheimer. He established a number of secret laboratories where some of the most brilliant scientists in the world gathered to build a nuclear weapon before the Axis powers could build their own. The Manhattan Project was a success, though it unleashed a terrible, destructive force on the world that continues to haunt us to this day.

Hiroshima and Nagasaki

At approximately 8:15 AM, August 6, 1945, the United States dropped a nuclear bomb on the Japanese city of Hiroshima. World War II was winding down, but Japan refused to surrender. The United States hoped to force it to do so with a show of overwhelming and terrifying force.

The Japanese city of Hiroshima was completely destroyed by a single nuclear weapon. This image shows the remains of Hiroshima.

The effects of the bomb were immediate and horrifying. The blast from the explosion leveled most of the city, instantly killing tens of thousands of people. Those nearest the spot where the bomb was dropped were immediately vaporized.

People farther away suffered serious or lethal burns, and many were disfigured for the rest of their lives. Others received lethal doses of radiation. Dust and ash from the explosion rose into the atmosphere and then rained down on the city. Survivors described this fallout as "black rain."

On August 9, 1945, a second nuclear weapon was dropped on the Japanese city of Nagasaki. The Japanese government soon surrendered to the Allies. World War II was over. In Hiroshima, the death toll from the initial blast and its aftereffects eventually rose to approximately two hundred thousand. In Nagasaki, approximately 140,000 people were killed. Both cities were completely devastated.

The Bomb's Terrible Power

The bombs dropped on Hiroshima and Nagasaki remain the only nuclear weapons ever used in an act of war. They were relatively small by today's standards. The bomb dropped on Hiroshima had an estimated yield of 15 kilotons, the equivalent of 15,000 tons of TNT. But even bombs this size are incredibly destructive.

The center of a nuclear explosion can reach temperatures of 10 million degrees Fahrenheit (5,555,538 degrees Celsius), hotter than the surface of the sun. In fact, the first bomb ever tested, in the desert of New Mexico, actually fused the sand of the desert into glass. The intense heat vaporizes nearly everything within a quarter mile (0.4 kilometers) of ground zero. The explosion is so bright that those who look at it directly suffer eye damage, sometimes blindness. The shockwave from the blast can kill every human being up to 1 mile (1.6 km) away from the explosion site.

This horrifying destruction can be accomplished by a 15-kiloton bomb. The largest nuclear weapon ever tested, the Soviet-made bomb Tsar Bomba, had an estimated yield of 100 megatons. This bomb was approximately 6,500 times more powerful than the bombs dropped on Hiroshima and Nagasaki.

The mechanical components of nuclear weapons may vary, but all contain either plutonium or certain types of uranium. When plutonium or uranium is used to create an explosion, the energy released raises the temperature so much that it creates a massive blast wave. Nuclear explosions also emit electromagnetic fields, which can disrupt electric systems and devices. Thermal radiation is released, which causes a huge and destructive firestorm.

Uranium and plutonium are radioactive substances. As such, they can be harmful to plants and animals, as well as human beings. Nuclear radiation lingers on after the explosion has ended, contaminating land and water. Radiation from many American and Soviet nuclear tests in the 1950s and 1960s can still be detected today. In the event of a nuclear war, radiation could remain in the environment and poison survivors. Radiation poisoning, also known as radiation sickness, is characterized by nausea, vomiting, diarrhea, and hair loss. If serious enough, it can result in seizures, coma, or even death. The long-term effects of radiation exposure can include cancer and sterility, which is the inability to have children.

Some scientists have speculated that a so-called nuclear winter could occur in the event of a massive nuclear war. Dust and ash from numerous nuclear explosions could block enough sunlight to lower Earth's temperature and create a murky, perpetual winter. Others have speculated that atmospheric nuclear explosions (explosions detonated high above the planet's surface) could seriously deplete Earth's ozone layer. This would further expose survivors to illness — primarily sunburns, sun poisoning, and skin cancer.

If one nuclear weapon could destroy thriving cities like Hiroshima and Nagasaki, what could a hundred nuclear weapons do? Or a thousand? What about eight thousand? Could nuclear weapons destroy every single human being on Earth? This question became a serious concern in the period following World War II, when former allies the United States and the Soviet Union became the world's preeminent superpowers and bitter rivals.

The Cold War

The Union of Soviet Socialist Republics (USSR), or Soviet Union, was a Communist country that existed from 1922 to 1991. Existing in Europe and Asia, the USSR was comprised of present-day Russia, as well as fourteen surrounding countries. The United States and the USSR were huge countries with large populations, and they had conflicting political philosophies. After World War II, both the United States and the

During the Cold War, the United States was very concerned about a potential Soviet nuclear attack. These schoolchildren hide under their desks in a 1951 air raid drill.

USSR tried to become the world's most important super-power. Although the two nations did not engage in direct conflict, they began amassing weapons for a possible future clash.

This arms race, known as the Cold War, was especially serious because the United States and the Soviet Union developed massive stockpiles of nuclear weapons. At their peak, the USSR had approximately forty-five thousand nuclear weapons, and the United States had approximately

A. Q. Khan

Abdul Qadeer Khan was born in India in 1936. He moved to Pakistan as a young man. Later, he traveled to Amsterdam, the Netherlands, to work at a research laboratory. While there, Khan stole classified documents from the lab. After his return to Pakistan, he was chosen to head his country's nuclear program. Pakistan set up a nuclear laboratory as early as 1976 and tested its first nuclear weapons in 1998.

Khan was not content with simply working to improve Pakistan's nuclear infrastructure. It is believed that, by the mid-1980s, he began exporting nuclear components. At this time, it is thought that Khan secretly cooperated with Iran, working to build that nation's nuclear program. Evidence also indicates that he tried to sell Iraq a nuclear weapon in the late 1990s. It appears that Khan also began working with Libya and North Korea, earning millions of dollars. He even had brochures printed up advertising his services. But by 2001, the Pakistani government had forced him to retire. In February 2004, Khan made a public confession about his activities. He was placed under house arrest but was released in 2009. Pakistan had little interest in severely punishing the man who helped build its nuclear program, keep pace with its sworn enemy India, and raise its international stature and influence as a nuclear state.

thirty-two thousand. For decades, the citizens of both nations lived in the very real fear that, one day, they might awaken to the sound of air raid sirens, alerting them that certain destruction was headed their way.

In 1991, the Soviet Union collapsed, breaking up into fifteen separate countries. Just like that, the Cold War was over. But the United States and the USSR were left with thousands of nuclear weapons. These weapons were still very deadly.

Proliferation

The United States and the USSR constitute two out of nine nuclear weapons states. In Europe, both England and France are nuclear weapons states. China has nuclear weaponry, a technology it pursued after the Soviet Union "went nuclear." India followed soon after, as did Pakistan, India's neighbor and rival. North Korea recently became a nuclear weapons state, testing its first nuclear weapon on October 9, 2006. Israel is known to have nuclear weapons, although no one is exactly sure what the size of its stockpile is. Currently, Israel is the only nuclear weapons state in the often volatile Middle East, although Iran may soon join it unless the international community can convince that nation to give up its nuclear ambitions.

It seems that as more countries develop nuclear weapons, more want them. More countries with nuclear weapons means there is a greater chance that nuclear weapons may someday be used. Global politics are always changing, and countries that are at peace today may be at war tomorrow. Any war between nuclear weapons states could result in nuclear war.

Unsecured Nuclear Material

It is believed that some unaccounted for nuclear weapons exist around the world, primarily in the former Soviet Union. Should such weapons fall into the hands of an aggressive nation or terrorist group, the consequences for the world could be very dire.

The process used to create nuclear power is not far removed from the process used to create nuclear weapons. Any nation with working nuclear power plants already has nearly everything it needs to manufacture a nuclear weapon. Nuclear power plants also contain materials that can be stolen and used to make nuclear weapons. Waste from nuclear power plants can be used to create dirty bombs. Terrorists might target nuclear facilities in an attempt to destroy them or steal nuclear materials that could be made into weapons. While every nuclear power plant in the United States has a security force, most would not be up to repelling a determined group of trained soldiers, armed to the teeth and intent on breaking in and stealing radioactive material.

Chapter 2

WHAT IF? NUCLEAR ANNIHILATION SCENARIOS

These missiles are on display as part of a military parade in India. One of the most populous nations in the world, India is a nuclear weapons state.

The very idea of nuclear war is terrifying. But could it lead to the end of the world? Could nuclear war really annihilate, or destroy, all life on Earth? Realistically, what is the worst that could happen?

A full-on nuclear war could destroy millions of people, erase entire cities from the face of the planet, cause terrible damage to the environment, invite long-term health problems like leukemia and cancer, and permanently change the course of human civilization.

If nuclear war is so dangerous, why would anyone ever use a nuclear weapon? Even though it seems that no objective could be worth such devastation, consider how many people have been killed in the last one hundred years by conventional weapons. According to Robert McNamara, the U.S. secretary of state under presidents John F. Kennedy and Lyndon B. Johnson, an estimated 160 million people were killed in wars and other violent conflicts in the twentieth century. That's roughly equivalent to half the population of the United States. It's possible that even more people will be killed in violent conflicts in the twenty-first century, without the help of nuclear weapons. If nuclear weapons are used, these numbers could be much, much higher.

Nuclear Terrorism

The increase in terrorist activity around the world has given rise to fears of nuclear terrorism. Unlike nation states, which must protect their interests abroad and at home, terrorist groups are not worried about damaging their public image. They also can't be held to international treaties. Terrorist groups are difficult, if not impossible, to negotiate with, and they work independently from the countries in which they are based. Some terrorist groups may be made up of

These scientists are at work in Iran's Isfahan Uranium Conversion Facility. Iran is currently working to develop nuclear power, and many think that it may be attempting to develop nuclear weapons as well.

individual cells that have no knowledge of the activities of other cells within the group. This further complicates any attempt to target, deal with, or negotiate with a terrorist group, one that may have no central authority.

It is possible that terrorists could acquire a nuclear weapon and use it against civilian populations. Terrorist groups are generally comprised of people who hold extreme beliefs. Neither the group nor its beliefs and actions gain much public support. This is why terrorists are willing to resort to violence against innocent civilians—they aren't trying to gain popularity like most leaders and politicians are. If a terrorist group is willing to lose everything—even their lives—for their beliefs, they won't be deterred in their murderous actions by public outcry or persuaded to lay down their arms by attempts at diplomacy.

Proliferation

Various factors inspire countries to acquire nuclear weapons in the first place. Some countries want to acquire nuclear weapons for defense and security purposes. For instance, when India acquired nuclear weapons, rival nation Pakistan felt threatened and began developing its own nuclear program. Nuclear stockpiles are also an international symbol of prestige and influence. Very few countries are nuclear powers. Joining that group can be attractive for a country that wants to be taken seriously, to have a greater influence on world events, or wants a bargaining chip in international negotiations.

While most countries carefully monitor their nuclear material and keep it very secure, there are some nations that are not as careful. Unfortunately, it is possible that these unsecured nuclear weapons could fall into the hands of terrorists. The spread of nuclear material and weapons to other, previously nonnuclear countries is known as proliferation.

It is one of the gravest threats to global security in the twenty-first century.

Former Soviet States

The USSR had a large amount of nuclear material within its borders. This material still exists in Russia and the other countries that comprised the former Soviet Union. Some of this nuclear material is believed to be unsecured today. In a region that has undergone major political and economic upheavals in the past twenty years, it is possible that corrupt government and military officials might be willing to sell nuclear materials for a profit. While the Russian government won't acknowledge that any nuclear weapons have gone missing, they have admitted that some nuclear material has been stolen.

Pakistan

Pakistan, another recognized nuclear power, is also a politically divided country. It was once a part of its neighbor, India. In the decades since the two nations have been separated, there have been periodic clashes in border areas, and tensions remain very high between the two countries. Pakistan is also a predominantly Islamic nation, with a secular (nonreligious) government. There are political factions in Pakistan that would like the country to adopt a more hard-line, conservative, religion-based government.

Pakistani scientist A. Q. Khan sold nuclear secrets to Iran, North Korea, and Libya. It is believed that Khan's network was made up of many influential people, maybe even

This Indian soldier is engaged in a battle with Islamic militants in Mumbai, India. The militants took control of the Taj Mahal hotel, seen here. By the time the attack had ended, more than 150 people had been killed.

members of the Pakistani government. Also, it is known that terrorists, including Al Qaeda, are hiding in Pakistan. These groups would almost certainly love to acquire enough nuclear materials to make dirty bombs.

North Korea

An extremely repressive and authoritarian dictatorship, North Korea became a nuclear weapons state in 2006. Led by absolute ruler Kim Jong II, North Korea practices a severe form of communism in which its citizens are forced to live in extreme poverty and have no civil rights whatsoever. Financially mismanaged and estranged (isolated) from the rest of the world, North Korea has virtually fallen apart under Kim Jong II. Dependent upon humanitarian aid, it is believed that North Korea has been facing massive famines and malnourishment for years.

Unfortunately, Kim Jong II has spent a great deal of North Korea's scant capital on its military, including a nuclear weapons program. North Korea manufactures long-range ballistic missiles, which can deliver a nuclear payload over a long distance. North Korea has also withdrawn from the Nuclear Non-Proliferation Treaty, a major United Nations (UN) treaty designed to halt proliferation and monitor current nuclear states. Considering how desperate North Korea is for money, and how hostile it is to the idea of global cooperation and international law, it is very possible that it would be willing to sell nuclear materials or knowledge to terrorists intent on building a nuclear arsenal.

Iran

Iran, an Islamic nation actively working to acquire nuclear power, may also be building a nuclear weapons program. If Iran is soon able to make nuclear weapons, it may encourage other Middle Eastern nations to acquire them as well. Iran is known to fund Hamas, a fundamentalist Islamic organization based in the Palestinian territories. Hamas is dedicated to destroying Israel and replacing it with an Islamic nation. Hamas also has a history of using violent methods, including terrorism, to achieve this goal. If Iran is willing to support a terrorist organization financially, would it also be willing to supply such an organization with nuclear weapons?

Dirty Bombs

Not all nuclear weapons require advanced scientific knowledge to build. Nuclear material is very dangerous. Ordinarily, the by-products created at nuclear power plants are carefully monitored and disposed of. This nuclear waste is, by itself, dangerous enough to kill people.

If terrorists were to get their hands on nuclear waste, they could use conventional explosives like dynamite to create a dirty bomb that would disperse this radioactive waste. Used in a crowded city like New York, a dirty bomb could harm or kill many thousands of people within a small area. Moreover, it could contaminate the surrounding area where it was used, resulting in the illness or death of many others not affected by the initial explosion.

Dirty bombs could provide terrorists with a crude, but still very deadly, way to cause havoc and spread fear. The material used to build dirty bombs could be stolen from nuclear facilities anywhere in the world, including the United States.

Other Nuclear Terrorism Scenarios

Of course, if terrorists were to acquire or fashion a small-yield nuclear weapon—let's say, a 10-kiloton bomb, smaller than the bomb dropped on Hiroshima but much more powerful than a crude dirty bomb—the results would be much more frightening. If such a bomb was detonated in midtown Manhattan, it would destroy every building within a third of a mile (0.5 km) of the explosion. Buildings ranging

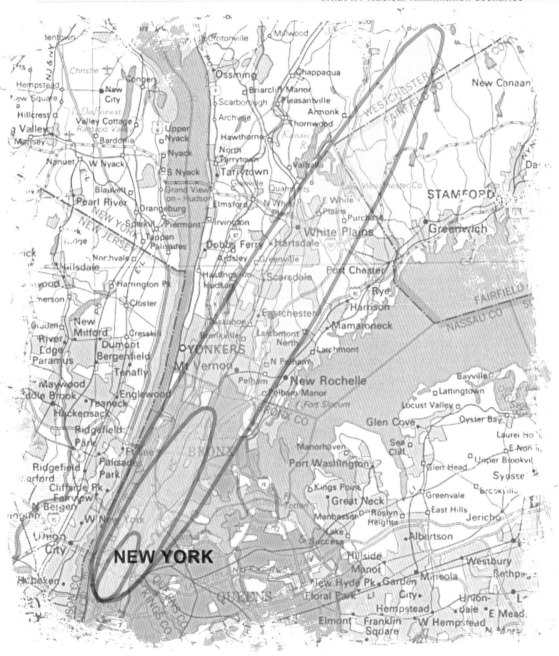

The destructive effects of a nuclear weapon are not solely limited to the immediate nuclear blast. This map illustrates how fallout might spread into upstate New York after an attack on New York City.

nearly a mile (1.6 km) from this circle of destruction would also be damaged. If this explosion occurred during an average workday, hundreds of thousands of people would be killed. Fires caused by the blast could affect structures within a mile and a half (2.4 km) of the epicenter of the explosion.

Assuming that the terrorist group that detonated the bomb could be identified, the United States—and, most likely, a coalition of its allies—might launch an offensive to hunt down and destroy the attackers. If these terrorists were hiding in a nuclear nation, such as Pakistan, things might become complicated. If the United States were to respond with nuclear force, it could be seen as a direct act of aggression against the country in which the terrorists were hiding. The use of nuclear weapons in this scenario would mark the first time since WWII that such weapons were used in an act of war. Unlike then, the United States is no longer the only nuclear weapons state in the world. The implications of this are clear: a U.S. nuclear attack could lead to a chain reaction of nuclear responses that could result in a large-scale, multiparty nuclear war with hundreds of devastated targets.

Even if a U.S. attack on a terrorist group's host country wasn't answered with nuclear force, the United States would not necessarily be free from further nuclear threats. Other terrorist groups might see the United States' use of nuclear force as a sign that they are morally and ethically free to respond with their own nuclear attacks (whether dirty bombs or a more sophisticated nuclear explosive). Or terrorist groups might step up conventional (nonnuclear) attacks on U.S. embassies, military installations, and civilians around the world. These terrorist attacks could spread to other countries, and U.S. allies could soon be dragged into a conflict with no clear boundaries or resolution.

Furthermore, should terrorist groups continue to carry out coordinated strikes on countries that are allied with the United States, it could set the stage for a multination conflict. A war between several nuclear weapons states would have the potential to move past conventional warfare to nuclear warfare. This would have extraordinarily serious repercussions.

Human Error

In 1995, Russian radar detected a Norwegian rocket. This rocket was not a weapon. It had actually been launched for research purposes. However, there was no way to tell that from the information relayed by radar. In fact, to the Russians, the rocket looked like a missile launched by a U.S. submarine! Fearing the worst, a countdown to a possible nuclear strike was initiated. Russian president Boris Yeltsin had it within his power to launch the brunt of Russia's considerable nuclear might at the United States. However, after slightly less than ten minutes passed, the Russians realized their mistake and stood down.

Although disaster was averted, this incident highlighted the weakness of our nuclear defenses. While we ponder global politics and conflict, we must also consider the fact that, with thousands of fully operational nuclear weapons around the world, simple error—rather than aggression and malice—might bring about nuclear annihilation. The chance that a nuclear weapon might be launched accidentally, precipitating a nuclear war, is very real.

Nuclear War Scenarios

The threat of nuclear war has hung over the world for more than sixty years. The horror of the bombings of Hiroshima and Nagasaki is almost too extreme for the human mind to comprehend. Thousands, perhaps tens of thousands, of such bombings within just a few days, hours, or even minutes of each other are unthinkable—but definitely possible. How could a full-on conventional war between two nuclear-capable nations lead to such an event?

India and Pakistan

Neighboring rivals India and Pakistan have managed to acquire approximately one hundred nuclear weapons between themselves. India tested its first nuclear weapon in 1974, and Pakistan conducted its first nuclear test in 1998. Pakistan broke away from India in 1947, and the two nations have had tense relations ever since. The dominant religion in Pakistan is Islam; in India, it is Hinduism. The two nations have clashed over territory before, and some worry that future clashes could escalate into nuclear war.

Besides the extensive destruction that a nuclear war would cause to both nations, there is a danger that a nuclear conflict between India and Pakistan could spread to other

India and Pakistan have clashed over disputed territory numerous times since the two countries split apart in 1947. This creek marks the border between these neighboring atomic powers.

countries. Islamic extremists outside the region might begin targeting Indians. Or terrorists might use the war to recruit supporters in Pakistan and elsewhere to spread chaos and conflict more widely.

North Korea and South Korea

North Korea is believed to have a very small nuclear arsenal, which it developed with the assistance of A. Q. Khan. Although a very poor nation, North Korea heavily invests its scant financial resources in its military, which contains approximately one million soldiers.

The formerly united nation of Korea was split into two countries after WWII. South Korea became allied with the United States, and Communist North Korea became allied with the Soviet Union. In 1950, North Korean troops invaded South Korea. Within three years, a cease-fire was declared, but the war between the two states has never officially ended.

North Korea has few allies and has proved remarkably resistant to diplomatic efforts to disarm its nuclear program and draw it back within the international community. U.S. president Barack Obama has expressed a desire to open up diplomatic relations with the secretive country, but only on the condition that it discontinues its nuclear weapons program. North Korea refuses to do this. North Korean officials claim to have enough plutonium for four or five nuclear weapons.

South Korea maintains strong alliances with the United States and Japan, and both countries would certainly stage a military intervention if North Korea attacked South Korea. Though North Korea is a tiny and impoverished nation, the sheer size of its army would guarantee a long and difficult war.

Iran and Israel

Israel is the United States' strongest ally in the Middle East. The tiny nation has gone to war with its neighbors many

Iranian president Mahmoud Ahmadinejad is a controversial leader. He has used aggressive rhetoric when discussing Israel, even declaring that it should be "wiped off the map" or destroyed.

times over the years. It is the only nuclear weapons state in the region. Recently, Mahmoud Ahmadinejad, president of Iran, has made it very clear that he opposes the existence of Israel.

Iran is attempting to develop nuclear power. Any country with a functioning nuclear power plant could also make a nuclear weapon. In fact, on March 1, 2008, Admiral Mike Mullin, of the Joint Chiefs of Staff, stated on CNN's *State of the Union* that the United States believes Iran currently has enough uranium to make a nuclear weapon. However, he added that the country is still a long way from being able to build a nuclear stockpile.

Israel is a very small country. In fact, it is approximately the size of New Jersey. Just a few nuclear weapons could wipe out all of Israel's major cities. Since Israel is a nuclear weapons state, a first strike by Iran would almost certainly prompt an Israeli nuclear counterstrike.

Южная Осетия

A nuclear war between Iran and Israel could drag other nations into a larger war. An Iranian nuclear strike on Israel could invite U.S. or UN intervention. If Israel counterattacked Iran with a nuclear weapon, it is very likely that Iran's allies would rally to support it. Suddenly, a far larger war between the West and the East could erupt. The Middle East, long a powder keg of regional

Since the breakup of the Soviet Union, there has been sporadic conflict between former Soviet territories. This Russian news footage shows a Georgian tank in Tskhinvali, Georgia, destroyed by Russian forces.

and global tension and conflict, could finally explode. The devastating results would affect nearly every nation in the world, even those far from the region and politically neutral. It would be nuclear Armageddon.

The United States and Russia

For decades, the United States and the Soviet Union were adversaries. Emerging as the world's two great superpowers following WWII, both nations began stockpiling nuclear weapons. For decades during the Cold War, these countries teetered on the brink of nuclear conflict.

Today, following the breakup of the Soviet Union, Russia remains a massive political power. Struggling with political and economic changes, Russia is no longer a Communist country. But it is also not a true democracy. As the largest nation in the world, Russia is still very powerful, and it is actively trying to expand its strength and influence.

While the United States and Russia are currently not adversaries, the two nations disagree on many political issues. At one time, both had vast nuclear arsenals aimed at each another. Even though the Cold War is over, little has changed. Should both countries ever come into direct conflict again, it's possible that they could quickly revert to their old patterns of distrust and hostility. The conflict could escalate into a full-on nuclear war.

Chapter 3

OBSTACLES TO DOOMSDAY

These French police officers stand at the ready as a shipment of weapons-grade plutonium arrives at a factory.

Fear is a powerful emotion. When contemplating nuclear war, there is much to be fearful of. While many events could spark a nuclear conflict, the likelihood of a nuclear war ever occurring is relatively slim. There are a number of obstacles standing in the way of such a conflict breaking out.

The chances of nuclear terrorism happening are relatively low. Thankfully, it isn't easy for terrorists to get their hands on nuclear weapons. Actually building a nuclear weapon requires a great deal of specialized knowledge and equipment. It's very unlikely that any terrorist group would have the resources or know-how to build such a bomb.

There are many other compelling factors that argue against worst-case nuclear annihilation scenarios, including technical hurdles, dwindling nuclear stockpiles, international oversight and agreements, international sanctions, and shifting political attitudes toward both nuclear weapons and membership within the international community.

Technical Hurdles

More than 99 percent of the world's nuclear material is accounted for and protected by heavy security. Plutonium is very rare and would be extraordinarily expensive to

Atoms for Peace

In 1953, U.S. president Dwight D. Eisenhower delivered his "Atoms for Peace" speech to the UN General Assembly. In it, he put forth a bold vision of a future in which atomic power would be used for peaceful purposes and the arms race put to an end: "The United States would seek more than the mere reduction or elimination of atomic materials for military purposes. It is not enough to take this weapon out of the hands of the soldiers. It must be put into the hands of those who will know how to strip its military casing and adapt it to the arts of peace. The United States knows that if the fearful trend of atomic military buildup can be reversed, this greatest of destructive forces can be developed into a great boon, for the benefit of all mankind."

purchase. Weapons-grade uranium is similarly rare and expensive. Standard uranium can be "enriched," or made into the kind of uranium that can be used to create a nuclear weapon. But again, this process requires specialized knowledge and precision equipment. Enriching uranium is not only beyond the capabilities of a terrorist group, but it is beyond the capabilities of most countries. Should a terrorist group purchase or steal highly enriched uranium (HEU) or plutonium, they would be faced with the difficulty of how to actually work with it. Both of these substances are radioactive and very dangerous, even deadly.

Unsecured nuclear weapons, such as those believed to be in the former Soviet Union, also present a set of problems for a terrorist group or rogue nation. Like many other complicated pieces of machinery, nuclear weapons require regular maintenance, or they will cease to work properly. It is possible that, should a terrorist group purchase a stolen nuclear weapon on the black market, it might not still be in working order. Also, most nuclear weapons come equipped with complex safeguards that prevent unauthorized individuals from detonating them.

Reduced Nuclear Stockpiles

The number of nuclear weapons in existence reached its apex during the Cold War. Since then, the United States and the former Soviet Union have greatly reduced their nuclear stockpiles. As a result, there are fewer weapons for terrorists to attempt to get a hold of. And, in the event of nuclear war, fewer nuclear weapons could be used. In fact, since the late 1980s, the number of nuclear weapons in the world overall has steadily declined. The United States and Russia have made a concerted effort to reduce the size of their stockpiles. Some nations have agreed to do away with their nuclear programs altogether.

Out of all the countries that have the technological and financial capacity to build or acquire nuclear weapons, very few have actually done so. Most nuclear-capable nations have found that the costs of having such weapons far outweigh the benefits.

International Oversight and Agreements

The United Nations' International Atomic Energy Agency (IAEA) carefully monitors all nuclear materials. Established in 1957, the IAEA is an organization dedicated to promoting peaceful uses for nuclear energy and preventing the proliferation, or spread, of nuclear weapons worldwide. To this end, the agency and its director, Mohamed ElBaradei, were recognized by the Nobel Institute in 2005, when they were awarded a Nobel Peace Prize.

One of the most important functions the IAEA performs is monitoring nuclear material. The Nuclear Non-Proliferation Treaty, or NPT, was designed by the IAEA to stop the spread

The United Nations International Atomic Energy Agency (IAEA) is responsible for keeping an eye on nuclear materials, weapons, and infrastructure around the world. Here, IAEA scientists inspect a nuclear plant near Baghdad, Iraq.

of nuclear weapons. It was put into effect in 1970. Countries that sign the treaty agree to submit to intensive IAEA inspections regarding their nuclear activities. Safe, peaceful nuclear power and technology are generally more useful to nations than nuclear weapons are. The IAEA helps countries improve nuclear safety and security. It works to prevent nuclear materials from falling into the hands of terrorists. The IAEA also works to stop the illegal procurement (obtaining) and sale of nuclear materials.

Currently, about 160 nations have signed the NPT and are working alongside the IAEA to ensure that they have safe and peaceful nuclear futures. Nations that refuse to cooperate with the IAEA may face sanctions and other punishments from the international community.

International Sanctions

For new and aspiring nuclear weapons states, a number of outside factors make it unlikely that they will ever use these weapons because doing so would be against their own best interests. International sanctions—penalties that restrict trade in commercial, medical, military, and even humanitarian goods to the rogue nation—are the primary tool used to deter countries from developing, testing, or using nuclear weapons.

Because North Korea manufactures long-range ballistic missiles, its nuclear developments have left many nations around the world uneasy. On March 2, 2009, Japanese

North Korea increasingly finds itself both isolated and impoverished. Here, North Korean children are fed at a nursery in the capital, Pyongyang. North Korea is dependent on international aid to feed its citizens.

Prime Minister Taro Aso informed the North Korean government that additional tests of long-range rockets would prompt the UN Security Council to apply more sanctions against North Korea. North Korea has already suffered greatly under sanctions. Further economic and humanitarian sanctions would be detrimental—even catastrophic—to the isolated, impoverished nation.

Shifting Political Attitudes

While the threat of nuclear war is real, the world has changed considerably since the days when Americans were terrified of the possibility of the Cold War escalating into a global nuclear apocalypse. Nuclear weapon stockpiles have been decreasing for more than twenty years. Most nuclear countries are members of the United Nations and voluntarily submit to international supervision of their stockpiles. Those that don't are locked into a number of international alliances that they would be reluctant to damage. Strict nonproliferation protocols have ensured that the world has relatively few nuclear states.

For the great majority of countries, it's more advantageous to avoid nuclear weapons than to acquire them. Currently, there are no worldwide conflicts being waged that could conceivably precipitate a full-out, multistate nuclear war. For all the fighting that has occurred in the world since the invention of the nuclear bomb, people and governments have demonstrated that they are unwilling to use nuclear weapons—at least so far.

Chapter 4

PREVENTING NUCLEAR ANNIHILATION

Preventing the spread of nuclear weapons requires international cooperation. Here, the International Commission on Nuclear Non-proliferation and Disarmament holds its first meeting in 2008 in Sydney, Australia.

We know that nuclear weapons are dangerous. So what is being done to stop their use? The development and proliferation of nuclear weapons has been carefully monitored since the dawn of the Atomic Age. If this hadn't been the case, we could very well be living in a world with many more nuclear states than exist today. Reducing the number of nuclear weapons states helps prevent the chance of nuclear war. Reducing the chance of a full-out nuclear war revolves around a few simple principles.

Nonproliferation

When nations have acquired nuclear weapons for national security purposes, they have often done so in response to a rival nation that has nuclear weapons. Having nuclear weapons transforms the relationship between countries and inevitably sparks further proliferation, increasing the chance of a nuclear conflict. This process must be stopped if we are to avoid nuclear annihilation. In fact, the single best way to lessen the chance of nuclear war is to make sure that new countries don't get nuclear weapons. Every country has its own group of allies and enemies. These relationships should be governed by careful, reasoned diplomacy — not blunt nuclear intimidation.

Disarmament

Stopping proliferation is one important step to achieving a world that is free of nuclear weapons. Actually reversing proliferation takes the world one step closer to a nuclear-free future. Some countries have voluntarily given up nuclear weapons.

For instance, throughout much of the second half of the twentieth century, South Africa was a deeply unpopular country because of its racist government policies known as apartheid (which were formally ended in 1994). Having begun to develop nuclear power under the Atoms for Peace program in 1957, South Africa eventually began to develop nuclear weapons. Ultimately, the nation decided that it would be to its benefit to cooperate with the IAEA. In 1991, it officially joined the NPT as a nonnuclear weapons state. South

North Korea's unpredictable government is developing long-range missiles, like this one test-launched on April 5, 2009, which could potentially be outfitted with a nuclear warhead.

SOLON MIDDLE SCHOOL

Africa believed that it would be more secure without nuclear weapons, so it disarmed its missiles.

Aggressive Oversight

The IAEA's role in preventing nuclear conflicts can hardly be overstated. Fewer countries have nuclear weapons in the twenty-first century than at any point from the 1960s through the 1980s. In addition, the number of nuclear weapons worldwide has been more than halved since 1986. Only four nuclear countries—India, Pakistan, Israel, and North Korea—haven't signed the NPT.

An overwhelming majority of world governments have signed the NPT, a fact that is not to be dismissed lightly. The public's perception of nuclear weapons has changed greatly since the Cold War. More people and their governments see them as a source of danger instead of security. Most people wish to see their elimination, rather than their increase and proliferation. It seems unlikely that this trend will reverse itself.

If North Korea and Iran agree to completely renounce nuclear weapons and fully cooperate with the IAEA, it is very possible that a long-lasting era of nonproliferation can be brought about. The incentives offered to these countries by the UN to encourage them to end their programs are considerable, as are the negative consequences if they continue to pursue these dangerous weapons.

Securing Loose Nuclear Material

Securing loose nuclear materials is one of the most significant actions that can be taken to reduce the likelihood of

Study War No More: No Nukes!

After the breakup of the Soviet Union, once sovereign nations that had been swallowed by the USSR regained their independence. Three of these newly independent countries—Belarus, Kazakhstan, and Ukraine—found that they had nuclear weapons left over from the USSR. Between them, they had approximately four thousand nuclear weapons. Like South Africa, they also decided that they would be better off without nuclear stockpiles, so they got rid of them.

Other nations that have ended their nuclear weapons programs include Libya, Brazil, and Argentina. Their new lack of nuclear weapons has not compromised these nations' security or damaged their reputation within the international community. If anything, their statures have risen since they sacrificed their nuclear arms for the greater good and security of the world.

Currently, there are fewer countries with long-range ballistic missiles than there were during the Cold War. These missiles can be fitted with nuclear warheads and used to attack nations on the other side of the world. The number of ballistic missiles in the world has declined by more than half since the mid-1980s.

nuclear terrorism. Efforts to tackle this issue have included the Nunn-Lugar Soviet Nuclear Threat Reduction Act of 1991, which allocated funding for securing nuclear materials in former Soviet states.

Contact Us | S

IAEA.org
International Atomic Energy Agency

About IAEA   Our Work   News Centre   Publications   Data Centre

» Interactive Timeline

The IAEA in Time *Decisive Years*

Highlights & Previews

- General Conference 2008
- IAEA & Iran in Focus
- Scientific Forum Reports & Presentations
- World News Headlines

52nd IAEA General Conference
29 Sep - 4 Oct 2008, Austria Center, Vienna

Nuclear Power for the 21st Century

16 April 2009 | International cooperation on initiatives such as the International Project on Innovative Nuclear Reactors and Fuel Cycles (INPRO) is crucial for the future of a global nuclear system. Full Story »

The International Atomic Energy Agency (http://www.iaea.org) finds peaceful uses for nuclear energy and promotes nuclear security. Without its efforts, nuclear weapons could be more widespread than they are today.

Further action can, and should, be taken. Holding the United States and the world up to stricter nuclear security standards would be a crucial step toward preventing nuclear terrorism. Nuclear materials can, and should, be

extremely heavily guarded to prevent their theft.

International Cooperation

The world we live in today is more interconnected than the world of sixty years ago. Globalization is transforming business and culture. New technologies allow people thousands of miles away from each other to communicate easily and effectively. Music, film, television, fashion, theater, and other artistic forms are instantly disseminated all over the world. The world is more open than it used to be, a process that will inevitably continue and have ramifications for political cooperation.

Through international cooperation, we can ensure that warfare doesn't go nuclear. We can be aware of the nuclear capabilities of every country. We can encourage each nation to keep track of its nuclear arsenals and ensure that, should standing nuclear treaties be violated, those responsible will be brought to justice. Preventing the use of nuclear weapons is every nation's responsibility.

In addition, individual countries can be encouraged to devote time and resources to rooting out terrorist organizations within their borders. Terrorist cells have to depend on some larger group or collection of individuals for funding.

Even the most secretive terrorist networks can be identified, located, and disrupted.

It is also important for every nation to play by the rules set down by the NPT. A lot of international attention has been focused on the four nations that have not signed this treaty—Israel, North Korea, India, and Pakistan. But it's also important that those countries that have signed the treaty do not violate it. The NPT can only work if it is respected. So far, it has done much to prevent nuclear proliferation.

Successful international cooperation hinges on every country playing by the same set of rules. One of the biggest incentives for militarily weak nations to sign the NPT is that nations with powerful militaries, and, in some cases, nuclear weapons or the potential to make them, have signed it as well. If international treaties like the NPT aren't respected by its signatories, they can break down. This is why open, honest cooperation and fair play are necessary if we ever hope to rid ourselves of these dangerous weapons.

What You Can Do

In the United States, we are lucky to have our democratic freedoms, civil liberties, and civil rights. The right to free

Many people who are opposed to nuclear weapons have made their voices heard. These Hawaiian protesters demonstrate against nuclear tests being carried out in the South Pacific.

speech, the right to free assembly, and the right to vote gives individual citizens a great power. But with this power comes responsibility. Ultimately, you are responsible for helping determine the future of the world. If you want to live in a world without the threat of nuclear war, you have the power to work to make that happen.

It is never too early to learn more and think about ways to get involved. Joining the student government; volunteering at nonprofit organizations devoted to peace and nonproliferation; and lobbying local, state, and government officials about nuclear issues are just some of the ways that you can get involved in the political process and add your voice to the debate. Many colleges offer classes in political science, human rights, and international relations. You can even major in these and related subjects and launch yourself into a career in which you fight on the front lines to create a world that is finally free of the specter of nuclear annihilation. It is never too soon to get involved in shaping the world that you would like to live in and hand over to your children.

air raid siren A siren that alerts the civilian population to an incoming assault by air.

amass To gather, collect, hoard, or stockpile.

ambition The strong desire to attain a certain goal or fulfill a purpose.

annihilation Complete and utter destruction.

ballistic missile A missile fitted with a warhead that is capable of delivering its payload over a great distance.

contaminate To poison.

conventional explosives Nonnuclear explosives.

devastated Having suffered terrible destruction.

disrupt To break up or interrupt.

fallout The radioactive dust and other debris spread into the atmosphere after a nuclear explosion. Fallout often enters the atmosphere and then returns to Earth.

havoc Complete chaos.

humanitarian aid Assistance, such as food or medicine, provided to a needy country for humanitarian, or life-saving and life-sustaining, purposes.

nausea A feeling of sickness.

negotiate To bargain with.

perpetual Unending, or continuing for an indefinite amount of time.

sanctions A series of economic punishments, such as fines or trade restrictions.

shockwave A forceful disturbance created by a blast.

sterility The state of being unable to reproduce.

vaporize To change into a gas.

volatile Unstable or explosive.

For More Information

Carnegie Endowment for International Peace
1779 Massachusetts Avenue NW
Washington, DC 20036-2103
(202) 483-7600
Web site: http://www.carnegieendowment.org
This nonprofit organization is dedicated to fostering peace by
promoting international cooperation.

Center for Arms Control and Non-Proliferation
322 Fourth Street NE
Washington, DC 20002
(202) 546-0795
Web site: http://www.armscontrolcenter.org
This nonprofit, nonpartisan organization works to increase
global security.

International Atomic Energy Agency (IAEA)
1 United Nations Plaza, Room DC-1-1155
New York, NY 10017
(212) 963-6010
Web site: http://www.iaea.org
The IAEA monitors nuclear materials around the world in the
interest of promoting peaceful uses for nuclear energy.

Nuclear Threat Initiative
1747 Pennsylvania Avenue NW, 7th Floor
Washington, DC 20006
(202) 296-4810
Web site: http://www.nti.org

The Nuclear Threat Initiative is dedicated to reducing the threat of weapons of mass destruction by strengthening global security.

Union of Concerned Scientists
2 Brattle Square
Cambridge, MA 02238-9105
(617) 547-5552
Web site: http://www.ucsusa.org
This nonprofit organization is dedicated to finding ways to apply science and technology toward solutions, rather than to military purposes.

United Nations (UN)
First Avenue at 46th Street
New York, NY 10017
(212) 963-4475
Web site: http://www.un.org
Headquartered in New York City, the UN was established in 1945 to promote international security, cooperation, human rights, and economic development.

Web Sites

Due to the changing nature of Internet links, Rosen Publishing has developed an online list of Web sites related to the subject of this book. This site is updated regularly. Please use this link to access this list:

http://www.rosenlinks.com/doom/nucl

For Further Reading

Baker, David. *Biological, Nuclear, and Chemical Weapons: Fighting Terrorism*. Vero Beach, FL: Rourke Publishing, 2006.

Brezina, Corona. *Public Security in an Age of Terrorism*. New York, NY: Rosen Publishing, 2008.

Cothran, Helen. *Do Nuclear Weapons Pose a Serious Threat?* (At Issue). Farmington Hills, MI: Greenhaven Press, 2004.

Friedman, Lauri S. *Nuclear Weapons and Security*. San Diego, CA: ReferencePoint Press, 2007.

Gerdes, Louise I. *Nuclear Weapons* (At Issue). Farmington Hills, MI: Greenhaven Press, 2009.

Maus, Derek C., ed. *Living Under the Threat of Nuclear War*. Farmington Hills, MI: Greenhaven Press, 2005.

Mayell, Mark. *Nuclear Accidents*. San Diego, CA: Lucent Books, 2003.

Minneus, Steve. *Nukes: The Spread of Nuclear Weapons*. New York, NY: Rosen Publishing, 2008.

Orr, Tamra B. *Iran and Nuclear Weapons* (Understanding Iran). New York, NY: Rosen Publishing, 2009.

Phillips, Tracy A. *Weapons of Mass Destruction: The Threat of Chemical, Biological, and Nuclear Weapons* (Issues in Focus Today). Berkeley Heights, NJ: Enslow Publishers, 2007.

Sheen, Barbara. *Nuclear Weapons* (Ripped from the Headlines). Yankton, SD: Erickson Press, 2007.

Bibliography

Baidi, Mubashir, and Laura King. "A. Q. Khan, Pakistani Nuclear Scientist, Freed by Pakistan Court." *Los Angeles Times*, February 6, 2009. Retrieved February 2009 (http://www.latimes.com/news/nationworld/world/la-fg-pakistan-khan7-2009feb07,0,4151948.story).

Carnegie Endowment for International Peace. "A. Q. Khan Nuclear Chronology." CarnegieEndowment.org, September 7, 2005. Retrieved February 2009 (http://www.carnegieendowment.org/static/npp/Khan_Chronology.pdf).

Centers for Disease Control and Prevention. "Acute Radiation Syndrome." CDC.gov. Retrieved February 2009 (http://www.bt.cdc.gov/radiation/ars.asp).

Cirincione, Joseph. *Bomb Scare: The History and Future of Nuclear Weapons*. New York, NY: Columbia University Press, 2007.

Hodgson, Martin. "North Korea Has Plutonium Ready for Up to Five Nuclear Bombs, Reports Claim." Guardian.co.uk, January 17, 2009. Retrieved February 2009 (http://www.guardian.co.uk/world/2009/jan/17/northkorea-south-korea-nuclearweapons).

International Atomic Energy Agency. "IAEA Primer: Maximizing the Contribution of Nuclear Technology to Society While Verifying Its Peaceful Use." IAEA.org. Retrieved February 2009 (http://www.iaea.org/Publications/Factsheets/English/iaea-primer.pdf).

Jenkins, Brian Michael. *Will Terrorists Go Nuclear?* Amherst, NY: Prometheus Books, 2008.

Leventhal, Paul L., Sharon Tanzer, and Steven Dolley, eds. *Nuclear Power and the Spread of Nuclear Weapons*. Dulles, VA: Brassey's, Inc., 2002.

Mo, Richard. "Author Sees Greater War Casualties." *Daily Pennsylvanian*, June 14, 2001. Retrieved February 2009 (http://media.www.dailypennsylvanian.com/media/storage/paper882/news/2001/06/14/News/Author.Sees.Greater.War.Casualties-2160801.shtml).

Oppenheimer, J. Robert. *The Open Mind*. New York, NY: Simon & Schuster, 1955.

Riminton, Hugh, Richard Roth, Barbara Starr, and Susie Xu. "U.N. Slaps Trade, Travel Sanctions on North Korea." CNN.com, October 15, 2006. Retrieved February 2009 (http://www.cnn.com/2006/WORLD/asiapcf/10/14/nkorea.sanctions/index.html).

Shanker, Tom. "U.S. Says Iran Has Material for an Atomic Bomb." *New York Times*, March 1, 2009. Retrieved March 2009 (http://www.nytimes.com/2009/03/02/washington/02military.html?_r=2&hp).

Younger, Stephen M. *Endangered Species: How We Can Avoid Mass Destruction and Build a Lasting Peace*. New York, NY: HarperCollins, 2007.

Index

About the Author

Frank Spalding is a writer and editor who lives in New York. He has written several books for Rosen Publishing concerning geopolitics and warfare, including *Genocide in Rwanda* (Genocide in Modern Times). Spalding has long been fascinated by global politics, international diplomacy, and the arms race.

Photo Credits

Cover (top), p.1 © U.S. Air Force/Time & Life Pictures/Getty Images; cover (bottom), p.1 © www.istockphoto.com/Denis Jr. Tangney; pp. 4–5 © Greg Mathieson/Mai/Time & Life Pictures/Getty Images; p. 7 CBS/Photofest; p. 9 © Steve Crise/Corbis; pp. 10–11, 12–13 © AFP/Getty Images; pp. 16–17 © Bettmann/Corbis; p. 21 © Daniel Berehulak/Getty Images; pp. 22–23, 35 © Behrouz Mehri/AFP/Getty Images; p. 26 © AP Photos; pp. 32–33 © Chris Hondros/Getty Images; pp. 36–37 © Channel One/AFP/Getty Images; p. 39 © Jean-Paul Pelissier/Reuters/Corbis; pp. 42–43 © Ramzi Haidar/AFP/Getty Images; pp. 44–45, 49 © AP Photos; p. 47 ©Torsten Blackwood/AFP/Getty Images; pp. 54–55 © Newscom.

Designer: Sam Zavieh; Photo Researcher: Marty Levick